Welsh Jokes

by

CHRISTIE DAVIES

jjc JOHN JONES CARDIFF LTD.

WELSH JOKES

First published, March 1978

Reprinted, May 1978

ISBN 0 902375 45 8

Design by Neil Barber
Setting by Afal, Caerdydd
Illustrations by Gren
Printed by Salesbury Press, Llandybie

JOHN JONES CARDIFF LTD.
41 Lochaber Street,
Cardiff
CF2 3LS.

CONTENTS

page

1. An Englishman, a Scotsman, an Irishman . . . and a Welshman!

A wealthy man left legacies to three of his friends on condition that when he was buried, they each placed £5 in his coffin. When he died, the first of his friends, who was an Englishman, dutifully placed a £5 note in his coffin; the second friend, an Irishman, added £5 in pennies which he had saved up for the occasion. The third friend, a Scotsman, removed all the money from the coffin and replaced it with a cheque for £15 made 'payable to bearer'. Unfortunately for Sandy one of the bearers turned out to be a Welshman and he promptly cashed it.

* * * *

A group of Welshmen travelling home by train from Paddington became very merry in the bar and at regular intervals were heard to cheer 'Hurrah for Wales'. A morose Englishman stood this for some time but finally turned towards them and retorted loudly "Hurrah for Hell'. 'Fair enough', replied the Welsh, 'every man for his own country.'

* * * *

In America they put woman on a pedestal but in Wales they've put her on their national flag.

* * * *

At an international eisteddfod it was customary for one representative of each of the competing countries to be present on the platform at the opening ceremony. Half an hour before it was due to start the organising committee were horrified to find that there was no representative of England present. Looking desperately round the field the chairman saw a man at the edge of the crowd who looked like a typical Englishman and ran up to him to explain the situation. The stranger listened and then replied in a strong Welsh accent 'I'm sorry I can't help you. I'm not English at all. I was sick on the bus getting here.'

* * * *

A Welsh geologist has claimed that Wales is bigger than England because of its hills. If Wales were rolled out as flat as England, it would be the bigger country of the two.

An Englishman, a Scotsman, an Irishman and a Welshman were travelling in an aircraft that went out of control and was about to crash. To their dismay, they discovered that there were only three parachutes in the plane. The Scotsman argued that he ought to have one since he was a very important businessman whose death would result in the collapse of the stockmarket. The Welshman handed him over the first parachute and he baled out. Next the Irishman argued that he should be given a parachute. He was an important politician upon whom all hope of peace in Ireland rested. The Irishman silently put the straps over his shoulders and he jumped out after the Scotsman. The Welshman now turned to the Englishman and handed him a parachute. 'Here you are' he said cheerfully. 'But what about you?' gasped the Englishman, amazed at this unflinching heroism. 'Oh, I'll be all right' said the Welshman. 'The Irishman took my haversack'.

* * * *

A certain political appointment once lay between a Welsh and a Scottish M.P. An Englishman was asked who he thought should get the job. 'Well,' he replied, 'if we get the Welshman he'll pray on his knees on Sundays and on his neighbours the rest of the week. If we get the Scotsman we'll keep the Sabbath and anything else he can lay his hands on.'

* * * *

The Welsh Catholics claim that they invested Saint Patrick in the Bank of Ireland over 1,500 years ago and are now drawing the interest in Irish priests working in Wales.

* * * *

In America the ethnic elite are known as the Wasps, the White Anglo-Saxon Protestants. The equivalent group in Wales are known as the Traditional Welsh Protestants.

* * * *

2. Crafty and Naive

Welsh receptionist to visitor: "I'm afraid the chairman is out, but if it is really important he'll see you."

* * * *

During the controversy over the disestablishment of the Church of Wales the two chief protagonists were David Lloyd George and the Bishop of St. Asaph. On one occasion Lloyd George addressed a meeting in a small Welsh village where he was introduced by one of the deacons of the local chapel as follows "We all know the remarks made on this subject last week by the Bishop of St. Asaph who, in my opinion, is the biggest liar in creation. Fortunately we have here tonight Mr. David Lloyd George who will be more than a match for him."

* * * *

A man walked into a pet shop in Merthyr and asked to buy a thousand cockroaches. "A thousand cockroaches!" gasped the shopkeeper, "what on earth do you want with them?" "Well", said the customer, "I'm moving out of my old house today and the lease says I must leave the premises exactly as I found them."

* * * *

A customer who had ordered some Welsh lamb from her butcher, suspected that the meat she had been given was not the genuine article. "Are you sure this is real Welsh lamb?" she demanded, angrily. "Well, Mrs. Jenkins", confessed the butcher, "that lamb was really born in New Zealand but I can assure you it had Welsh parents."

One Welsh trader to another: "I'm not calling you a liar. I'm merely saying that if you and I were in business together, we'd tell more lies than any two people ever before, and I'd be silent."

* * * *

Advertisement in Welsh hairdressers': "Before using your hair tonic I had three bald patches. Now I have only one."

* * * *

A Welsh hill farmer had a small farm with just a few sheep. One day while his wife was dyeing a bedspread a little lamb fell into the bucket of dye and emerged bright blue in colour. A passing tourist seeing the blue coloured lamb bought it for fifty pounds. The farmer saw he was on to a good thing, so he dyed all his other lambs in bright colours and sold them at a vast profit. With the money he made he bought up all the lambs in the county and now he's the biggest lamb dyer in the whole of Wales.

* * * *

An English visitor to a small Welsh village was approached by one of the deacons of the local chapel who asked him whether he would like to attend their chapel on the following Sunday. "Wouldn't that be a little pointless?" replied the Englishman. "After all, your services are held in Welsh and I don't understand the language." "Ah yes," said the deacon, "but the collection is in English."

* * * *

Nosey woman: "Do you find it a profitable thing to keep a cow?"
Jenkins: "Oh yes, my cow gives about eight quarts a day."
Woman: "How much of that do you sell?"
Jenkins: "About twelve quarts."

* * * *

David Lloyd George, when Chancellor of the Exchequer, was once addressing the House of Commons on the Insurance Bill. Some M.P.s complained that because Lloyd-George was facing the Chair with his back to the majority of members they could not hear what he said. "There is my difficulty", replied Lloyd-George, "I have been told to address the Chair." "Address the Chair", came the reply, "but speak in this direction." "That," said Lloyd George, "would involve something that I never do — facing both ways."

3. Names and ancestors

Some names from Wales:

(i) The man with only two teeth left and those in the front of his mouth — Dai central eating.

(ii) Cardiff strip club owner — Aaron the G string.

(iii) The village gossip you can never get rid of: Mrs. Jones thestay-maker.

(iv) After H.G. Wells discovered that Oliver Cromwell's real name was Williams and that his ancestors came from Margam, he always referred to the great man as "Williams-the-conqueror".

(v) The local chiropodist — Williams the corn-curer.

(vi) A Welsh physicist — Dai-atomic.

(vii) A reckless risk-taker — Huw ap Hazard.

* * * *

An Englishman travelling on a very dark night in the Welsh mountains heard a cry for help from someone who had fallen into a ravine near the road. "Who is it?" he replied cautiously, fearing a trap. "Dafydd ap Gwilym ap Rhys ap Gruffydd ap Ifan ap Jenkyn" came the response. "Well", rejoined the Englishman, "if there's half a dozen of you down there you can jolly well pull one another out."

* * * *

A Russian spy was dropped by parachute in the Welsh hills with instructions to contact a Mr. Jones who lived in the small village of Llanfair, and give him the code message "the tulips are blooming well today." Arriving at the village he asked a small boy where Mr. Jones lived and was directed to a small cottage at the end of the village. He knocked on the door and the owner emerged. "Are you Mr. Jones?"

"I am."

"The tulips are blooming well today."

Mr. Jones stared at him in amazement and then smiled. "Ah, you must have come to the wrong house. It's Jones-the-spy you want."

* * * *

A head teacher had a very poor memory for names and could not even remember the names of his own staff. He had what he thought was a very clever way of covering up this defect. "Let me see," he would say. "How do you spell your name?" Sometimes this worked, but it failed dismally with the Welsh science master who craftily suggested he write it down carefully. The headmaster took out his pencil and notebook and the science master then slowly and carefully articulated the letters J - O - N - E - S.

* * * *

Two men who arrived late at a crowded theatre in Cardiff could not find a seat and had to stand at the back. Getting tired after the first act, one of them shouted loudly at the beginning of the interval "Mr. Evans's house is on fire." They immediately had the choice of nineteen vacant seats.

* * * *

Dai Jones predeceased his wife by several years, so when she died, she asked St. Peter if her husband was there. "Well", said St. Peter, "we've got thousands of Jones's here, what's his first name?" "Dai", said Mrs. Jones, "Dai Jones." "We've got hundreds of Dai Jones's too," said St. Peter, "can't you identify him more specifically?" "Well," said Mrs. Jones, "before he died he said that if ever I was unfaithful to him he'd turn in his grave." "Oh, I know who you are looking for", said St. Peter, "your husband must be old Pinwheel Jones."

* * * *

If you ever wondered where all the Davies's come from, there's a big factory outside Bridgend with a sign outside saying "Davies Manufacturing Co. Ltd."

* * * *

One old Welsh family in Llandovery is very proud of its pedigree that covers five large skins of parchment. In the middle of the third page is a note in the margin "About this time the world was created."

4. Places and Holidays

A pupil describing in an essay his holiday in Aberystwyth, astonished and delighted his teacher by spelling the town's name correctly every time he used it. The next day the teacher asked him to the front of the class and said "Show the class how well you can spell. Write 'Aberystwyth' on the blackboard." "Please, miss, I can't any more," he pleaded, "I've eaten all my rock."

* * * *

A little old lady, visiting the seaside at Conwy for the first time, saw some men preparing to go fishing, collecting their baskets and nets. She said to one of them: "What are those things?"
He said "Lobster pots."
She said "Go on, you'll never train them to sit on those things!"

* * * *

Have you heard about the latest machine on the pier at Llandudno? You put ten pence in and ask it any question and it gives you a true answer. One holiday maker from Cardiff tried it last week. He asked the machine "Where is my father?" The machine replied: "Your father is fishing in South Wales." Well, he thought, that's daft for a start because my father is dead. "Where is my mother's husband?" Back came the reply, "Your mother's husband is buried in Cardiff but your father is still fishing in South Wales."

* * * *

Letter from Welsh Lodging-House Keeper: "I should like to know, please, whether you want two bedrooms with double beds in them, or two double-bedded rooms, as I have only one double-bedded room; all the beds are double beds except one in the double-bedded room, which is a single bed."

* * * *

Tourist in Barmouth: "Have you got anything in the shape of motor car tyres?"
Storekeeper: "Oh, yes. We've got lifebuoys, invalid cushions, funeral wreaths and doughnuts."

* * * *

A professor and his wife stayed on a farm in mid-Wales one

summer. They enjoyed it but were doubtful about going back there the following year because of the smell of the pig-sty next to the house. The professor wrote to the farmer about it and the farmer replied: "We haven't had any pigs on the farm since you were here last summer. Do come again."

* * * *

When you can see the coast of Devon from Swansea it is going to rain. When you can't, it is raining already.

Two old ladies from Liverpool on holiday in Colwyn Bay decided to have their photograph taken by a beach photographer. Having posed them suitably he disappeared under his old-fashioned black hood behind the camera. "What's he doing now?" asked one of the old ladies, timidly. "Oh, he's going to focus", replied the other. "What, both of us?"

* * * *

A little old lady in Tenby earned her living by selling tea and cakes to trippers from England. Being the daughter of a mean old South Gower farmer, she tried to boost her profits by using the same tea bags over and over again. At first no one noticed and she made a lot of money. The word got around that her tea wasn't what it used to be, the trippers stopped coming and she went out of business. Moral: Honest tea is the best policy.

It is now over ten years since the last train stopped at the railway station with the longest name in Britain — Llanfairpwllgwyngyll-gogerychwyrndrobwll-Llantysilio-gogogoch in Anglesey. When a train stopped at the station the porter would cry out "Anybody in there for here?"

★ ★ ★ ★

Sign outside a cafe in Rhyl. "Fish and chips 40p. Children 20p."

★ ★ ★ ★

And the latest news from the Glamorgan county cricket ground at St. Helen's in Swansea: Two and a half inches of rain have fallen for seven runs.

An Englishman on holiday in Penmaenmawr was told that the chapel had driven all the loose women out of the village, but that they still operated in caves up in the mountain at the back. "It's very simple", said his Welsh informant, "you go up there and shout yoo-hoo-hoo outside the cave. If there is no answer then she is busy, but if she shouts yoo-hoo-hoo back, you go in and negotiate." That evening the Englishman climbed up to the cave and shouted but there was no reply so he decided to go back to the pub. On the way back he came across another big cave at the foot of the mountain so he went to the entrance and shouted yoo-hoo-hoo as loud as he could. Yoo-hoo, yoo-hoo-oo-oo-oo replied the cave. Full of excitement, the Englishman rushed into the dark entrance and was run over by the express train for Holyhead.

The 'little trains of Wales' are famous for going up steep hills but they don't all have powerful engines. On one railway train, the engine is so weak that when the driver blows the whistle it stops the engine.

* * * *

A group of English tourists climbing in Snowdonia came across a shepherd sitting at the top of the hill watching over his sheep. "I suppose you can see a great distance from here on a clear day," said one of the tourists. "Yes, indeed," said the shepherd seriously, "on a clear day you can see five television regions. "I suppose on a clear day now you could see as far as London from this great altitude," said one of the climbers, nudging his companions. "Oh, you can see much farther than that," said the shepherd. "Further than London?" gasped the tourists. "Oh, yes, further than America even." "Further than America?" shouted the climbers, "that's impossible."
"Well," said the shepherd, "if you don't believe me, just you sit down here for a couple of hours and if the clouds will clear you'll see the moon.

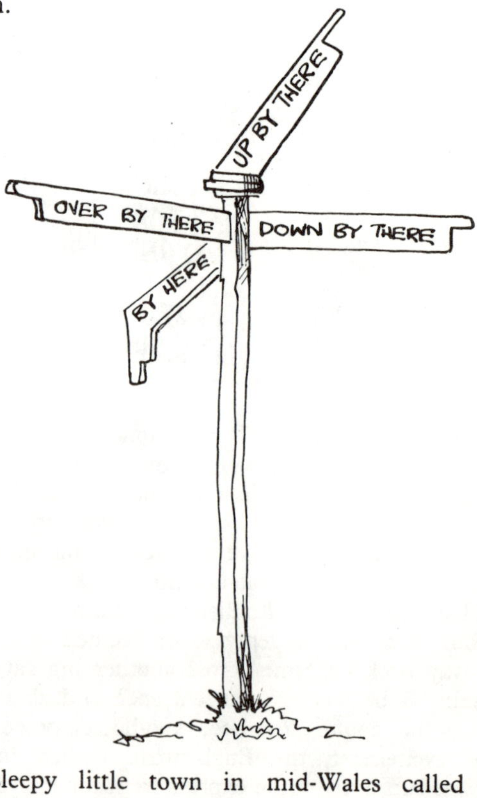

There's a sleepy little town in mid-Wales called Llandyfnod.

5. Words and Phrases

Father: "Now Baby say Dad, Da-da-da"
Mother: "Come on baba, say Mam, Mam-mam-mam"
Baby: "D-d-damn."

* * * *

First Welshman: "How are you, I hope?"
Second Welshman: "Thank you, no doubt."

* * * *

A witness in a court case in North Wales was asked if he would like an interpreter. "No sir," he replied emphatically, "I speak two spokes."

* * * *

A Welshman was loosing a golf match until his opponent badly sliced a crucial shot. "Ah", he exclaimed, "I'm afraid you're in the bunker, I hope."

* * * *

Three Welshmen in a pub praising the beer:
First Welshman: "Best glass of beer I never tasted no better."
Second Welshman: "So did I neither."
Third Welshman: "Neither did I too."

* * * *

Two Welshmen travelling at night from Blackpool to Bridgend got into an empty compartment at the end of the train and went to sleep. Later the train stopped suddenly at a station and woke them up. "Dai, have a look out of the window and see where we are," said Will. Dai looked out. "Oh, we're in Cheltenham", he said. "That's all right", said Will, "we don't have to change until Cardiff." An hour later the train stopped again, and again Will asked Dai to look out for the name of the station. Dai again said it was Cheltenham. "Funny", said Will, "I didn't know there were two Cheltenhams." A third time the train stopped. "Cheltenham again," said Dai. "Come off it, there can't be three Cheltenhams", said Will, "let's have a look" . . . "Get away, mun, that's not 'Cheltenham', it's 'Gentlemen'."

"Yes", said the proud mother, "our Evan is up in London learning pharmacy."
"Well, he needn't have gone all that way," replied Mrs. Jones the farm, "he could have come to our farm to learn and welcome."

* * * *

Welsh Landlady: "Don't call them jugs, Mari, they are ewers."
Maid: "Oh, thank you Mrs. Morgan, and are all these basins for me too?"

* * * *

Notice outside London theatre: "The part of the Welshman has been filled. The Dai is cast."

* * * *

A visitor to Llanrwst asked a local resident to direct him to the house of Mr. Evan Griffiths. The reply was: "You see those two houses at the top of the hill? Well, Mr. Griffiths lives in the middle one."

* * * *

Two women in Splott were having an angry argument on the pavement when the daughter of one of them popped her head out of the window and shouted "Quick! mam, call her a thief before she calls you one."

* * * *

Road sign in North Wales: "Yes, you can't!"

* * * *

One morning an inspector went into a Welsh school, entered a class and took over the lesson on the resurrection of Lazarus. "Now children," he said, "what is the English for Mair?" Immediately a forest of hands shot up and the answer Mary was given.
"What," continued the inspector cunningly, "is the English for Martha?" No-one answered and then one nine year old raised his hand. "Mrs. Davies sir", he said.
"Why do you think it is Mrs. Davies?" asked the inspector in astonishment.
"Well, sir," came the answer, "everyone calls the lady who lives in Rose Cottage 'Mrs. Davies,' but her husband calls her Martha.

6. Welsh logic and argument

Welsh debator: "I have listened with great care to my opponent's speech this evening and I would like to congratulate him on the impeccable logic of his argument. Unfortunately the factual premises on which he based his case are quite clearly false. Now if you combine false premises and faultless logic you must come to a conclusion that is definitely incorrect. I fully admit that the factual assumptions on which I shall base my argument are just as likely to be wrong as those of my opponent. But I intend to make mistakes in the logic of my argument and so I have at least a random chance of being right. The probability of my opponent being correct is zero, but I have a small but finite chance of coming to the correct conclusion. Therefore you must support me on mathematical grounds alone."

* * * *

A Welsh school-inspector visiting a small village primary school was struck by the great resemblance between two small girls sitting at the front of the class.
"You must be twins", he exclaimed.
"No we are not", replied the little girls firmly.
"Well then," said the inspector to the first girl, "how old are you?"
"Nine years and two months."
"And how old are you?" he asked the other girl.
"Nine years and two months."
"Then you definitely must be twins."
"No we aren't, we're all that's left of triplets."

* * * *

Political Arithmetic.
Canvasser for Liberal Party: "Will you support the Liberals this time?"
Welsh Mathematician: "No that is impossible. In the past the Liberal Party occupied a position between the left wing of the Conservative Party and the right wing of the Labour Party. Then the left wing of the Conservative Party moved further left and the right wing of the Labour Party moved further right, so the Liberal Party was squeezed out until ultimately it had to perform the difficult task of inserting itself between two coincident points. Since the Conservatives went on moving left and the Labour Party went on moving right the Liberals now occupy what is mathematically an imaginary point in space. How can I vote for an imaginary party?

7. Politics and Local Government

The earliest Welsh politician of whom we have detailed evidence is Old King Cole (Coel). Even he had at least three fiddles on the side.

* * * *

A West Glamorgan councillor was recently accused of providing council jobs for no fewer than eighty-three of his relatives. He hotly denied this and pointed out that only eighty-two of his kinsmen were employed by the council. His relatives have now moved a motion of censure against him for his carelessness in missing one of them out.

A Welsh M.P. has justified the rise in the price of platform tickets on the grounds that we now get a longer wait between trains.

* * * *

When Asquith lost his seat in a General Election, he was offered a safe Liberal seat in Wales. He curtly refused, saying "I would rather go to Hell than go to Wales." It is widely believed that his wishes in this matter were completely carried out.

* * * *

Motto of the hangers-on to powerful Welsh councillors: "Servility costs nothing."

The chairman of a Welsh education committee was so illiterate he couldn't read even the clearest handwriting. On one occasion he was given a letter by a messenger who noticed that, after opening it, the councillor was holding it upside down and scanning it. "If I may say so Alderman Jones," said the messenger, meekly, "you're holding that letter the wrong way up." The Alderman replied with indignation "Do you think I could have obtained my present position as chairman of the education committee if I couldn't read a letter with any side up whatsoever?"

* * * *

The Chairman of a Welsh education committee called one of his junior officials into his office at County Hall. "How are you getting on now?" he asked him kindly. "Is everybody treating you well in the office and are you fitting yourself for better things?"
"Oh, I think so," said the young official modestly.
"Well," said the great man, "I'm going to make you Director of Education. What do you think of that?"
"I'm quite overwhelmed", said the youngster. "It really is good of you Dad."

* * * *

Welsh Alderman: "I have always tried to administer justice without swerving to partiality on the one hand or impartiality on the other."

* * * *

A civic function in South Wales was attended by many important London politicians. A policeman guarding the door had strict instructions to exclude all interlopers. The first person to arrive was a member of the present government. "You can't go in there without an authorisation" said the policeman, blocking the door against the great person. "But I'm a Cabinet Minister", spluttered the excluded one. "I don't care," said the policeman. "I can't let you in — Baptist, Methodist, whatever kind of minister you are."

* * * *

Welsh Labour orator: "I want you to realise that I am, if I may say so, but a fraction of the great working class."
Heckler: "Yes, and a vulgar fraction at that!"

* * * *

Plaid Cymru's policy for Welsh smallholdings: "Five acres and a Welsh-speaking cow."

The Labour caucus on a Welsh council held meetings in camera on the day before the full council meeting. Sometimes controversial issues were discussed and the party line laid down. Generally, however, the meetings discussed trivial issues at great length. On one such occasion a councillor having to leave early found the caretaker of the building fast asleep in a chair. "Wake up you scoundrel!" he cried, "you must have been listening at the keyhole."

* * * *

A Welsh headmaster had died and there were many applicants for the post. While the dead man was awaiting burial one of the applicants buttonholed the chairman of the education committee and asked "Would you have any objection to my taking the place of the headmaster?"
"No," replied the chairman, "not at all. Go and see the undertaker about it."

* * * *

8. Chapels, preachers and others

A prominent Welsh businessman on his death left his entire fortune to the local Chapel, having but rarely entered it while he was alive. The minister, when asked what he thought of the bequest, commented that it was the largest premium paid in fire insurance that he had ever known. "Even so," he added gloomily, "the risk is so great, I doubt the premium will cover it."

* * * *

In Wales the Methodists are divided into two groups, the galvanised methodists and the wee sly ones.

* * * *

The decline of the chapels in Wales — from dissent to absent.

* * * *

The night porter in a Welsh hotel saw to his surprise one of the guests coming down the stairs in his pyjamas at four o'clock in the morning. Tapping him on the shoulder he asked "What are you doing down here at this time?" The man started, and looking hazily at the porter replied: "I'm sorry, I'm a somnambulist." "I don't care what chapel you belong to", said the porter, "you can't go wandering round the hotel like this."

* * * *

An English geologist interested in the Ordovician rocks of mid-Wales saw an interesting outcrop while on a stroll through the countryside one Sunday. Taking out his pocket hammer he began to chip away at the exposed rocks. "What are you doing here?" demanded an old woman who had been watching him in amazement. "Can't you see, I'm breaking this stone", he replied. "You're doing more than that, you're breaking the Sabbath" came her retort.

* * * *

A Welsh preacher took as his text the passage from the Psalms: 'I said in my haste all men are liars'. "Yes", said the minister, "David said that in haste. But if he had lived here in Swansea he could have said it at leisure."

A Welsh clergyman who had received several calls to different chapels asked his wife where he should go. "Go where there is most sin, dear", advised his wife. The preacher took her advice and went to the chapel with the most money.

A gloomy lugubrious looking minister was travelling on a slow train across Wales with only one other passenger in the compartment. Suddenly he turned to his fellow traveller and demanded "Have you ever reflected that at any moment we may be launched into eternity?" "Yes", said the stranger, "many times." "And do you ever meditate on the great uncertainty of life?" "Yes, indeed, I think of this many times a day", replied the other.

"Indeed!" said the preacher, "can it be that I am talking to a fellow minister?"

"No," said the stranger, firmly, "you are not. I am a travelling agent for the London and Cardiff Life Assurance association. As it happens I have here a prospectus setting out the tables of mortality for clergymen and giving details of our special terms for ministers. And now, good-day to you sir, I must get off at the next station."

* * * *

In the Afan valley one of their many ruling passions is pigeon-flying. One ex-miner in the valley was visited when on his death-bed by the local minister who spoke to him about his future abode in heaven. "Do you expect to go there?" asked the dying man. "Yes," replied the minister. "And will you be an angel?" "Yes." "With wings?". "Yes." "And shall I also be an angel if I get to heaven?" "Yes," said the minister emphatically. "Well then, I'll race you for a pound!"

A Welsh preacher took as his text the parable of the five wise and five foolish virgins. Having explained at length the meaning of the parable and the fundamental moral choice implicit in it, he ended his sermon with a fine peroration and asked his congregation "And where would you rather be? With the wise virgins in the light . . . or with the foolish virgins in the dark?"

* * * *

A Rhondda coal-miner who had become a lay preacher one Sunday took as his text "For behold the darkness shall cover the earth and gross darkness the people" (Isaiah 60, 2). "When any of you miners are in the last seam and the lamp goes out, that's darkness", he said. "But what should we understand by gross darkness? Now when I was at school; I was taught that a gross is 144 and accordingly you will understand that gross darkness is 144 times darker than darkness."

* * * *

A Welshman was shipwrecked at sea and marooned on a desert island. When a passing vessel picked him up five years later the crew were amazed to find his little island covered in fine buildings that he had built himself. With pride the Welsh Robinson Crusoe took the captain round the island and pointed out to him his house, workshop, electricity generator and two chapels. "But what do you need the second chapel for?" asked the captain. "Oh, that's the one I don't go to," he replied.

* * * *

The beach evangelist at Borth-y-Gest was in full swing and denouncing his captive swimming-costumed audience, told them that "Hell is full of drink, gambling and loose women in suggestive bikinis." At this point a voice from the safety of the sand-dunes exclaimed "Oh death, where is thy sting!"

* * * *

The minister of a small village had lost his bicycle and suspected that one of the congregation had stolen it. One of the deacons advised the minister that the best way to catch the culprit was to preach a sermon on the ten commandments and to watch the faces of the congregation carefully when he got to 'Thou shalt not steal'. The minister began his sermon in fine style but lost the thread of his argument and ended the sermon in a complete muddle. "What went wrong?" asked his friend, the deacon, afterwards. "Well," said the minister, "the sermon was going well until I got to 'Thou shalt not commit adultery' and then I remembered where the bicycle was."

Mrs. Hughes was looking out of her front window one Sunday when she saw her neighbour coming up the drive dressed in his gardening clothes. "He must be coming to borrow our lawn-mower" she told her husband indignantly. "And on Sunday too. The very idea. Shameful. I won't let him have it. I'll tell him we haven't got one."

* * * *

Thomas Tudor and a few others had split off from their chapel because they could no longer accept the doctrines of their denomination. Some months later the minister asked Mr. Tudor whether he and the others worshipped together.

Tudor: "No, I found that they accepted certain points to which I could not subscribe, so I withdrew from Communion with them."

Minister: "So I suppose you and your wife carry on your devotions together at home."

Tudor: "Well, not exactly. I found that our views on certain doctrines are not in harmony so there has been a division between us. Now she worships in the North-East corner of the room and I take the South-West."

* * * *

There was an atheist in Cardiff that needed converting; so they took him to the rugby ground and kicked him over the posts.

9. Drink and Temperance

A farmer in one small Welsh village was regarded with some disfavour by the local chapel-goers because both he and his wife were heavy drinkers and indeed were known to drink beer out of the teapot. However, they were induced to attend a frenzied revival meeting in the chapel and were so affected by this that both of them gave up their intemperate habits. At the next meeting the farmer came forward to testify to the change in his life. "Yes," he declared, "the Lord has converted me, has converted my wife and has converted the teapot."

* * * *

Some sheep farmers in mid-Wales have formed a society of teetotalers. There is a clause in the rules that permits the use of alcohol at sheep-dipping time. One member keeps a sheep at home which he dips every day.

* * * *

A prominent Welsh minister travelling home one night was greatly annoyed when a young man much the worse for drink came and sat next to him on the bus. "Young man," he declared, "do you not realise you are on the road to perdition?" "Oh, Hell," replied the drunkard, "I could have sworn this bus went to Llanelli."

* * * *

10. Welsh Way of Death

"Today", wrote Megan in her diary, "I woke up feeling really depressed, but in the afternoon I went to Auntie Maggie's funeral and it cheered me up no end."

* * * *

Although it was some time since her husband died the Welsh widow remained inconsolable. To the insurance rep who came round to settle her late husband's policy she declared in tears "You know I'd give half this money to have my Evan back again."

* * * *

Soon after an unsuccessful Welsh trader died, his widow won a large sum on the football pools. One of the neighbours came round to congratulate her and remarked "What a pity it is that your Morgan can't share in your good fortune."
"Oh, but he will", declared the widow indignantly, "I'm paying to have him dug up from the back of the cemetery and moved to the front."

* * * *

An undertaker at a funeral was talking to a very old man from the next village. "Tell me," he said, "how old are you now?" "I shall be eighty-nine on my next birthday", was the reply. "Really?", said the undertaker, "it's hardly worth your going home, is it?"

* * * *

Definition of a Welsh peer: Senataff
Definition of a dead Welsh peer: Epitaff

* * * *

An elderly Cardi took his little grandson for a walk round the local cemetery. Pausing before one gravestone he said "There lies a very honest man. He died owing me £50 but he struggled to the end to pay off his debts, and if anyone has gone to heaven, he has."
They walked on a bit further and then came to another grave. The old man pointed to the gravestone and said "Now there's a different type of man altogether. He owed me £60 and he died without ever trying to pay me back. If anyone has gone to hell, he has."

The little boy thought for a while and then said "You know, Grandpa, you are very lucky."
"Why?" asked the old man in surprise.
"Well, whichever place you go to, you'll have some money to draw on."

11. A People Small in Stature Only

Lloyd George was once introduced to a meeting by a chairman who said "I had expected to find Mr. Lloyd George a big man in every sense but you can see for yourselves that he is quite small in stature."
Lloyd George: "In Wales we measure a man from his chin up. You evidently measure from his chin down."

* * * *

American news report: "On Saturday there was a great procession in New York of all the Welsh people in America. It was five miles long and five feet high."

* * * *

A diminutive Welshman was up before the magistrates in London charged with a sexual assault on a much larger Australian female. The magistrates were baffled as to how he had managed it and closely questioned the policeman who had arrested him.
"How on earth did he do it, officer?"
"He used a bucket, sir."
"You mean he stood on it?"
"No, sir, he put it over her head and swung from the handle."

12. Sex on the Hillside

Farmer Jones wanted to buy his neighbour's cow, but on enquiring the price he was shocked to learn it was £50.
"What", he protested, "here I am, your friend and neighbour, and you ask a price like that?"
"I'll tell you what", replied the other farmer, "seeing you are my neighbour I'll give you 20% discount."
Now Farmer Jones was not much of a scholar and he wasn't quite sure what this meant so he said "I'll think about it."
He went off down the road and was still trying to figure it out when he saw the local school-mistress coming towards him on her bicycle. He beckoned her to stop and said "Now tell me, Miss Pugh, if I were to offer you £50, less 20% discount, what would you take off?"
Miss Pugh thought for a moment and then declared "Everything, except my ear-rings."

* * * *

Dai, who had just turned 20, one day informed his father that he wanted to marry Mari the girl next door.
"I'm sorry, boyo," said his father, "but you can't marry her, you see as it happens she's your sister."
Dai was downcast but within a week he came back to see his father again. "Dad", he said, "I've made up my mind to marry Morfydd."
"Isn't that the girl behind the counter in Morgan's dairy?" asked his father . . . and it turned out she was his sister too. Gradually one after another the girls of the village were excluded from matrimonial alliance with Dai on the grounds of consanguinity (posh English for bloody relatives) until none was left.
One evening after the last girl had fallen under his father's interdict Dai was sitting in the front room looking sadly at the grate.
"What's wrong with you, Dai?" asked his mother, "girl trouble is it?"
"Yes, Mam," Dai replied, "every time I want to marry a girl, father makes out she's my sister."
"Oh, don't listen to that old fool", said his mother, "he's no relation of yours anyway."

* * * *

Dai had proposed to Megan and been accepted. "But", added Megan, before we get married I must tell you something dreadful about my past life."
"No," said Dai, "I won't hear of it. You can tell me after we're married."

After they were married and had set off for their honeymoon in Penarth, Megan again brought up the subject of her "dreadful secret". "No," said Dai, "it can wait. Tell me when we're in bed together, that'll be soon enough."
That night as they got into bed Megan declared "Well, Dai, now I really do have to tell you my secret. You see I'm a virgin." Dai didn't say a word but put on his clothes and travelled all the way back to his mother's house.
"Dai!" said his mother, "what are you doing here, you're supposed to be on your honeymoon."
"It's no good", said Dai, "I've had to leave Megan; it turns out she's a virgin."
"Well, Dai," said his mother, "in that case you were quite right to come home. If she's not good enough for the rest of the village she's not good enough for you."

* * * *

Mr. Lloyd approached the minister of his chapel after the service rather diffidently. "I have a difficult and delicate question to ask you," he said, "a question of religion which my wife and I cannot decide for ourselves. What we want to know is, is it right for us to indulge in marital sex on a Sunday?"
"Now that is a difficult question," replied the Minister. "I shall have to consult with the deacons about it."
A fortnight later the Minister called at the Lloyd's home.
"Oh, I am glad to see you" said Mr. Lloyd. "What was the decision you came to?"
"Well, we had a lovely meeting about it," said the minister, "the discussion went on for four hours."
"Yes, but what did you decide?"
"Mr. Lewis Williams spoke with great eloquence: he practically had me in tears", said the minister.
"Yes, but what . . ."
"And", the minister went on, "Mr. Griffiths-Jones gave us a most learned discourse quoting many wonderful thoughts from the scriptures."
"Yes, but what conclusion did you reach?"
"Oh, we decided it was all right, provided you didn't enjoy it."

* * * *

David Lloyd Geoge's amours were notorious, though curiously not damaging to his career. During the Great War his daughter Megan was trying to crash a bread queue in Wales.
"Who do you think you are?" cried the Welsh housewives.
"I'm Lloyd George's daughter", she said proudly, to which they all answered "So are we."

Plain nurse to pretty nurse: "Have you seen that Welshman in Ward 3 who is tatooed all over? I was giving him a bath this morning and I noticed he's even got LUDO tattooed on his you-know-what."
Pretty nurse: "That's not LUDO, that's LLANDUDNO."

* * * *

After Dai Jones got elected to the Council, he insisted on everyone calling him Councillor Jones. Coming back late from the pub after celebrating his election he made a great noise trying to get into his house. "Is that you Dai?" shouted his wife down the stairs. "Certainly not", he replied drunkenly, "it's Councillor Jones." "Well, come on up quick then, we've only got a few minutes before Dai comes back from the pub."

* * * *

First housewife: "Mary Pugh is getting married."
Second housewife: "Is she expecting a baby?"
First housewife: "No."
Second housewife: "There's a swank."

* * * *

Definition of a Welsh rarebit: A Cardiff virgin.

* * * *

The Bishop of St. Asaph and his wife were on holiday in Spain and were just signing in to their hotel in Seville. Now, although bishops of the Church in Wales have a title their wives are plain 'Mrs.'. So the good prelate wrote in the register "The Bishop of St. Asaph and Mrs. Williams." The hotel manager looked at the register in amazement and taking the Bishop to one side said "In Spain, Bishop, we are not as is commonly said, narrow-minded, and it is no concern of mine what your relationship is with this woman, but do you not think you could conduct this affair a little more discreetly?"

* * * *

13. Work and Play

"I hear Evan Morgan broke the world 100 yards record wearing mining boots."
"How did he manage that?"
"He fell down the shaft."

* * * *

Welsh health lecturer: "The two most debilitating diseases in Wales are silicosis and syphilis. Silicosis you get by going down a shaft . . . ."

* * * *

At an important Rugby match one man standing near the touchline was loaded down with expensive cameras, flashlight, telephoto lens — the lot. He made himself very unpopular with the crowd by chasing around after the play of the ball, obstructing everybody's view. Finally a voice from the crowd put an end to his antics by demanding "What else did you have for Christmas, Dai?"

* * * *

14. Cardiganshire meanness

Defninition of a Cardi: "A Scotsman robbed of his generosity." or "A man who can buy an item from a Jew, sell it to a Scotsman and make a profit."

* * * *

Two Cardis were chatting in the bus about which of their neighbours had died recently and how much money they had left.
First Cardi: "I see Will Evans has died, leaving £5,000 and he was well under sixty when he died."
Second Cardi: "It's strange how people die so much younger these days than they did in the Bible."
First Cardi: "Yes, I was only thinking yesterday that if Methuselah had been a good careful saver, he must have left a tidy sum of money when he died."

* * * *

A Cardi went into a chemist's shop and asked for fifty pence worth of arsenic.
"Fifty pence worth of arsenic?" said the chemist suspiciously, "what is it you want it for?"
"Thirty pence", replied the Cardi, innocently.

* * * *

Motoring tourist: "I'm sorry I ran over your hen. If I give you £5 would that be all right?"
Cardi farmer: "Better make it £10. I've got a cockerel that was very attached to that hen and the shock might kill him as well."

* * * *

A Cardiganshire man in his will left to his wife "all the goods in the bed, over the bed and under the bed."

* * * *

Have you heard of the Cardiganshire farmer who stuck a mirror to his dog's feeding bowl to make him think he was getting two bones for his dinner?

* * * *

Item in Cardiganshire hotel bill: Wear and tear of mirror — 10 pence.

Cardiganshire proverb — "There's one advantage in being poor. It's very inexpensive."

* * * *

Two men shared an old two-roomed farmhouse somewhere west of Tregaron. Dai grumbled to a visitor: "Rhys makes life unbearable at times. He keeps sheep and goats in the bedroom and it smells terrible."
"Why don't you open the window?" came the reply.
"What, and let all my pigeons escape?"

* * * *

First Cardi: "Didn't I see you at the travelling circus last week? Why didn't you take your little boy?"
Second Cardi: "He didn't have any money."

* * * *

Customer in a restaurant in Cardigan: "Don't you think this steak you've given me is a little thin?"
Waitress: "Don't be daft. If it was any thicker, you wouldn't be able to see the picture on your plate."

* * * *

When Captain Jones went to sea his family kept a light burning in the window for twenty years. When he finally came home they gave him a tremendous welcome and an electricity bill for £876.

* * * *

In Cardiganshire the local bread is so light in texture that a pound loaf only weighs eight ounces.

* * * *

A Cardi went into a chemists shop and asked for some sulphur. He was told it would cost him twenty pence. "Twenty pence!" he said angrily, "when I can get the same amount in Boots for only fifteen?" "Yes", said the chemist, "and you can go to another place and get as much as you want for nothing."

* * * *

One Cardiganshire farmer would never light a fire even in the middle of winter. Instead he used to suck a humbug and the rest of the family would sit round his tongue.

A tourist stopped to chat with a Cardi farmer who was putting up a building.
"What are you building?" he asked.
"Well, if I can let it", said the farmer, "it's a rustic cottage. And if I can't, it's a cow shed."

* * * *

A Scotsman and a Cardi met in Glasgow, both penniless, both thirsty. The Scotsman had an idea for getting a free drink: "I know a barmaid in a pub near here who has got a very bad memory. If you get her involved in a conversation she can't remember whether you've paid or not. Let me try it on first." The Scotsman went into the pub and duly got his free drink. Now it was the Cardi's turn to try. The Cardi went over to the bar, ordered his pint and began to tell the barmaid all about life in Wales. Ten minutes later he drained his glass and said to the barmaid "Well, it's been nice talking to you but I've got to be off now. What about my change?"

* * * *

Cardiganshire bill —
Item 1 Fresh egg (Markit Pryce) = 5p.
Item 2 Ware and tare of hen = 2½p.

The beaches in Cardiganshire seaside resorts are the safest in the whole of Britain. No one has ever drowned there from bathing after a heavy meal.

"Has that old Cardi farmer paid his bill yet?" asked the dentist's wife. "No", replied the dentist, "he not only refused to pay, he gnashed my own teeth at me."

* * * *

Cardiganshire coalman to his son: "Dai, what has your mam done with the new coalsacks?"
"She's made pillows out of them."
"What a waste of good sacks. Why couldn't she use the old ones?"

* * * *

An old Cardiganshire farmer had to go into hospital for an operation. As soon as he arrived at the hospital he was given a good bath. As he left the bathroom he said to the attendant: "Well, I'm gladd that's over. I've been dreading that operation for years."

* * * *

One old Cardi dairyman was so mean that after skimming his milk on the top, he used to look up and down the street from his shop and if there was no one around, he would turn it over and skim it on the bottom.

* * * *

At a typical Cardiganshire party, the main room is completely bare except for two bowls on the central table. As the guests arrive they place their false teeth carefully in one bowl and chew a walnut taken from the other.

* * * *

In answer to a written question the Secretary of State for Wales told the House of Commons that there had been eight cases of fraud in Carmarthenshire, twelve cases of fraud in Pembrokeshire, and two cases of attempted fraud in Cardiganshire.

* * * *

A note for Cardis — "You can't take it with you, and even if you could if would melt."

* * * *

A Cardi is a man who only cries over spilt milk if there's a water shortage.

Visitor to Cardigan seaside resort: "I want to buy a toothbrush".
Shopkeeper: "I'm sorry, but our summer novelties haven't come in yet."

* * * *

One year a Cardiganshire farmer had exceptionally good crops which he contemplated gloomily and declared: I'm sure such a great crop will put a terrible strain upon the land."